Halloween

A Guide to one of the World's Favorite Celebrations

Melinda Rolf

Introduction

Halloween only happens once a year—but is considered one of the world's favorite holidays, because it signifies fun and excitement. Both children and adults alike enjoy wearing scary costumes, attending themed parties, playing whacky games and eating quirky dishes.

But how exactly did Halloween originate and how is it celebrated in other countries? And, why are pumpkins connected to this holiday? Read on to find out

You will also discover how to make dishes, costumes, and create parties that will be the talk of the town on November 1st

Thank You and Enjoy!

Fun Halloween Facts

Halloween is a time of the year where ghosts aren't considered scary, and where you can have fun dressing up as your favorite monster, princess, super-hero, or movie character. It's also a time where kids can go "trick-or-treating", and when you can decorate your house with skeletons, mummies. Jack-O-Lanterns, spider webs and all those other fun creepy things.

But how exactly did it originate?

How it All Began

Halloween is actually the shortened term for "All Hallows' Eve", or "The .Night of the Dead". It was first coined in 1745, and was derived from the words "Hallow Evening", or "Holy Evening".

Halloween is celebrated on the 31st of October as the first in a series of celebrations called "All Hallow Tide", which is a time of the year that is dedicated to the dead—including martyrs, saints, and all the dearly departed. The holiday was created by Christians so that humor can be used in remembering the dead, and so that the fear of death can be lessened.

Research has it that this holiday was influenced by Harvest Festivals of the Celts, and that's why there has long been a debate whether it was started by Christians or not, because Celts are known as Pagans. However, some scholars believe that it was indeed started by Christians. This debate makes the celebration all the more interesting.

Customs

Pumpkin Carvings or Jack O' Lanterns

Possibly one of the most popular Halloween customs is the fact that pumpkins are carved with faces or shaped and are decorated with lights inside. These are called Jack O' Lanterns.

But did you know that turnips were the original crops that were carved? It all started with a Celtic Legend. In the legend, a man named "Stingy Jack" tricked the devil by turning the devil into a stone. This way, he was able to roam free around the world. However, he was not able to go either to heaven or hell. It was the devil's punishment, and because of that, he had to place coals inside carved turnips to give him light while traveling to get rid of other evil spirits. Since pumpkins are popular in the United States, and are easier to carve, people use them in place of turnips, especially during the Halloween season, to ward off evil spirits.

Wearing Costumes

The Celts started the idea of wearing costumes made from animal heads and skins to make them look like ghosts or demons, and so that the real evil spirits would not know that they were humans. Today, you can wear whatever costumes you like—whether they're scary or not!

Trick-or-Treating

This all started hundreds of years ago in Ireland. Apparently, during All Hallows' Eve, the poor would knock on the door of the rich and ask for alms. They could also ask for food. Today, this is usually done by kids donning their colorful costumes!

Animals Associated with Halloween

Many animals are connected to this holiday. Here are some of them.

Bats

Do you know why bats are often considered as scary creatures and why they're connected to Halloween? Well, that could be attributed to the fact that there are vampire bats around. Just like vampires who suck on Human's blood, vampire bats actually feed on the blood of other animals by cutting their throats with their teeth while the other animals are sleeping. Yikes!

Cats

Cats are usually associated with Halloween because they are "Familiars", or a witch's companions. It is even said that their magic is so powerful that they are the reasons why witches can protect themselves from other people. In Egypt, cats are considered as embodiments of gods, and are sacred.

Owls

In the middle ages, owls were feared because of the sounds that they made, and because they were considered as familiars of Athena, the Goddess of Wisdom. The most feared ones are Screech Owls, who were known to "scream like witches".

Spiders

Spider webs are often symbols of graveyards and haunted houses. People are also scared of the Black Widow Spider because she could cause one's death when she bites.

Toads

Remember Harry Potter's friend Neville Longbottom? He had a toad, right? Well, in ancient times, toads were considered as familiars of witches, too. They were also rumored to give off skin irritants, and that's why they are often feared.

Wolves or Black Dogs

When wolves or black dogs howl, people often say that they are able to see creatures, such as ghosts or demons, that the human eye cannot see—and that's why people should be scared of them.

Halloween around the World

Aside from trick-or-treating, and decorating the house with Jack O'Lanterns, there are other Halloween traditions around the world, too. Here are a few you might find interesting.

Bonfires in Ireland

Magicians in olden Ireland performed rituals so that the gods could be happy. They started bonfires, and often threw dead cattle to the flames, as a sacrifice for the gods. Bonfire is actually derived from the term "bone fires" that were made so that the gods would give farmers lots of sunlight so their crops would grow.

Austrians Leave Food on the Table

And not only that: they also leave a lighted lamp and some water on the table before going to bed on Halloween. This way, they get to attract the spirits of the dead and in turn, they will be provided with a lot of cosmic energy.

Tang Chieh in China

Basically, Tang Chieh stands for Halloween in China. During this holiday, they leave water and food in front of the photographs of their dead loved ones so that their journey in another world would be light and illuminated, and they will be able to find their way to heaven. Some families even invite monks so they could offer prayers and fruits for the dead.

Throwing Stones in England

Bonfires are also popular in England during this holiday. In fact, people throw stones, nuts, and vegetables into the fire to scare spirits away. They also sing the "Punkie Night Song", a traditional Halloween song. In the olden days, they also believed that if the stones that a person threw in the bonfire the night before disappeared, it meant that person would meet an early death.

Germans Hide Knives

The reason why Germans often hide their knives and other sharp objects during Halloween is the fact that they do not want the dead to be hurt while they visit the earth.

Japan's Obon Festival

Halloween in Japan is called the Obon Festival and during this holiday, bright red lanterns are placed all around the country. Bonfires are also lit so that the dead can find their way back to their respective families. However, instead of being celebrated on the 31st of October, this happens in July or August.

Visiting the Dead in Asia and Mexico

In Mexico, and in most Asian and Latin-American countries, it is customary to visit the dead once a year, from October 31 to November 2. People also place flowers, food, and drinks on the graves of their dead loved ones, and gather on the grave site as a means of remembering the dead and honoring them.

It's Party Time!

For the Kids: Make Halloween fun for kids with these party themes! Here are a few ideas to get you started.

Fairy Tale Party

Decorate the place with pumpkins, apples, and candies—reminiscent of the beloved fairytale, Hansel and Gretel. Ask the kids to dress up as their favorite Princes or Princesses, or other characters from various fairy tales, and give awards to the best or most creatively dressed kids—give them crowns, scepters, and capes so they will truly feel like royalty!

Harry Potter Party

One of the best ways to celebrate Halloween is by dressing up as characters from the Harry Potter Series. This way, kids could see witches and wizards not as scary, evil creatures, but as people who know how to have fun, and who are willing to save the world—in their own ways.

Decorate the house with cauldrons, have wands at the ready, and make sure that there are cobwebs all around, too. You can also buy mechanical owls or toads, and let cats roam around free, especially if no one is allergic to them. Oh, and don't forget to buy a standee of the troll who almost ruined Halloween for Harry and his friends! Dress up as Minerva McGonagall or Albus Dumbledore yourself and the kids will surely have a great time. "Expelliarmus!"

Alice in Wonderland Party

Make teatime fun! Spruce up your place with festive but muted colors, shadow cuts of characters from Alice in Wonderland, pictures of the Cheshire Cat, the flowers, and the caterpillar. Serve tea and cookies. (or biscuits as they are known in England) It'll surely be a classy and fun party for the kids!

Frozen Party

The movie still very popular these days and surely, kids would love to pretend to be Elsa, Anna, Hans, or even Olaf for a day! Decorate the place with snowflakes, reindeer, and ice castles. Serve frozen-themed cakes or cupcakes designed with the characters on them and the kids will surely appreciate you. Play songs from the movie or have Frozen karaoke

Monster Party

Decorate the house with characters from Monsters Inc, or other "not so scary" characters just let your creativity run wild and make monsters of your own.

Halloween Decorations

You can also make your own Halloween Decorations to make your place more inviting and interesting during the celebration. Here are some decorations that you can make on your own!

The Bat Chandelier www.mypapercrane.com

You will need:

Card Stock in black

Craft Paint in black

Scissors

Paintbrush

White Colored Pencil

Embroidery Hoops in small, medium, and large

Quilting Thread in black

Black Tape

Directions:

Paint all of the embroidery hoops black then draw bat shapes on the card stock using white colored pencil. You can also just download templates and trace them. Usually, you can make around 5 to 6 bats per page.

Then, attach thread through the embroidery hoops by securely tying each thread around each hoop. Hang the top tier of the hoop then add thread so you could attach the next tier, until you reach the third one.

Hang the bats by taping each bat to the string, starting from the bottom tier. Work your way upwards then hang the chandelier for everyone to see.

Crazy Cat Pumpkins

You will need:

2 fake pumpkins (you can usually buy these from craft stores, such as funkins.com)

Serrated sharp knife

Black acrylic paint

2 Styrofoam craft balls

Scissors

Paintbrush

Hot glue gun

Yellow, black, and pink felt paper

2 plastic or wooden toothpicks

11 pipe cleaners in black

a yard of decorative ribbon

Black yarn

Directions:

Remove the stems of the fake pumpkin by using a knife.

Then, paint the fake pumpkins black together with the Styrofoam balls and leave until dry.

Cut the eyes of the cat from yellow felt paper, its pupils from black felt paper, nose from pink felt paper, and ears from the black again. Use glue gun to attach the parts to the Styrofoam balls.

Then, cut the pipe cleaners in half to make whiskers.

Now, you can attach the head to the pumpkin. Do this by inserting a toothpick to the bottom of each head then insert the toothpick halves to the pumpkins using hot glue.

Make the tail by cutting the rest of the pipe cleaners in half. Twist each set together then secure with yarn. Use glue gun once more to attach to the back of the pumpkin.

Make a bow tie by cutting two ribbon lengths and attaching them together. Glue to the neck of the cats.

Voila! Your cat pumpkins are ready!

Papercraft Queen Elsa http://a.dilcdn.com

If you are going to make use of the Frozen theme, this will surely come in handy!

You will need:

A photo of Elsa from Frozen (you'll find lots in the internet! Just download and print)

Craft knife or scissors

Cardstock

Double-sided tape or glue

Cardboard

Directions:

After choosing a photo of Elsa, download it and make sure to print it on cardstock.

Fold Elsa's face a bit together with one side of her body so that she could stand. Make sure to fold in a direction that goes away from you, and not towards you.

Glue or use double-sided tape to let Elsa stand on a cardboard and display it wherever you want it to stay.

A Wreath Full of Spiders http://images.meredith.com

You will need:

Spiderweb fabric

Hot glue gun

Plastic spider

Embroidery hoop

Black ribbon

Directions:

Cover an embroidery hoop with spiderweb fabric. Use hot glue to keep it secure.

Then, use hot glue once again to attach the spider.

Use the black ribbon to form a bow around the hoop then hang it on your door.

My Free Gift to You

As a "Thank You" for downloading my book about Halloween, please accept this free book all about the raw food lifestyle. Please visit www.melindarolf.com to get your free book

Homemade Halloween Costumes for Kids

Dressing up is fun with these Halloween Costumes for kids that you can make on your own!

Ice Cream Sundae Costume

You will need:

Pink tank top

Velcro

Brown capelet

Headband

Fishnet fabric

Brown felt paper

Brown ribbon

Medium sized styrofoam ball

Pipe cleaners in various colors

Glitter glue

Directions:

For the headpiece:

Cut around 5 inches of brown felt and make sure that you make the edges wavy so they could resemble sauce. Around the edge, add some pleated brown trim then secure the ends with fabric glue.

Glue some quilt to the center to make whipped cream then cover with pipe cleaner then secure it with fabric glue.

Use glitter to cover the styrofoam then make sure to stick a red pipe cleaner on top to resemble a cherry stem. Attach the cherry to the center of the cream using hot glue then glue the whole headpiece to a headband.

For the dress:

Secure ends of capelet with velcro then cut an inch of pipe cleaner and attach them to the capelet with fabric glue.

Then, cut the bottom of the pink tank top to create a "dripping" effect and glue an inch of the pipe cleaner to make marshmallow sauce and attach it to the capelet with fabric glue.

Cut some elastic fishnet to make the cone bottom then attach it to the leggings by gluing the wasteband.

Skeleton Costume

Skeleton Costume http://cdn-image.realsimple.com

You will need:

White pleated ribbon

Scissors

Glue

Black long sleeved shirt

Black pants

Directions:

This one is pretty easy. Just cut the ribbon to pieces shown on the photo above and glue it to the shirt and pants to resemble a skeleton.

Owl Costume http://cdn-image.realsimple.com

You will need:

Glasses

Feathers

Cupcake Liners

Ribbon

Wire

Black or Brown Headband

Glue Gun

Brown Long Sleeved Shirt

Directions:

First, make sure to fold the cupcake liners in half then glue them to the shirt, from the bottom, all the way up. Create layers, just like what's shown on the photo above.

Then, make the cape by applying cupcake liners just like you did a while back. Layer lengthwise.

Glue some feathers on top of the glasses and on the sides, to resemble ears and to give your kid that "wise" look.

Halloween Treats for Kids

Kids are surely going to do a lot of eating during Halloween, so make it fun and unforgettable for them by making these treats!

Owl Pretzels (Meridith.com

Ingredients:

Large Pretzels (cooked)

Confectioner's coating

Black decorating sugar

Black jellybeans

Black licorice candies

Black licorice twists

Chocolate chips

Chocolate biscuits/cookies

Directions:

Prepare a bowl filled with confectioner's coating and dip the Pretzel there. Place it on waxed paper.

Then, sprinkle black decorating sugar onto the Pretzel while the coating is setting. Press jellybeans on the middle of the twist to resemble nose then place licorice candies at the bottom to resemble talons.

Next, separate a chocolate biscuit in half and place each on each side of the pretzel, as shown above and put white icing on the middle, followed by chocolate chips to resemble the eyes. Finally, add black licorice twists so the owl can have eyebrows, too!

Edible Frankenstein

Ingredients:

Shortbread or sugar cookie dough (cooked according to package directions)

Brown icing

Green frosting

Peanut butter cups

Your choice of candies

Directions:

After baking dough, cut out a variety of shapes from it then spread some green frosting on the cookies. Use brown icing and your choice of candies to create faces.

Add peanut butter cups to the sides of the cookies to resemble Frankenstein's head.

Enjoy!

White Meringue Mice (Meridith.com)

Ingredients:

1 tsp vanilla

2 egg whites

1/8 tsp salt

1/8 tsp cream of tartar

1 small tube of black decorating gel

80 pieces black licorice strings

Sliced almonds

¾ cup sugar

Directions:

In a medium bowl, let the egg whites stand for around 30 minutes in room temperature then pre-heat the oven to 325 F.

Then, add cream of tartar and vanilla to the egg whites, together with salt, then beat until soft peaks form using an electric mixer. Add a tablespoon of sugar at a time until stiff peaks form then pour meringue to an icing bag.

Pipe oval shapes to baking sheets. Make sure that one end is pointed to resemble faces of mice then bake the meringue mice for around 5 minutes and let them dry for around an hour.

Once the meringue mice are dry, it's time for you to decorate them. Use a small sharp knife to cut slits on top of each of their heads then insert sliced almonds into each slit. Cut a hole on the back using a toothpick so you could insert black licorice string for the tail. Then, pipe decorating gel for the eyes and nose.

Serve and enjoy!

Crispy Candy Corn (Martha Stewart .com)

Ingredients:

9 tbsp butter, unsalted and divided

¾ tsp fine salt, split into portions

12 cups mini marshmallows, divided

Red and yellow food coloring

1 Tbsp orange zest, grated

9 cups puffed rice crisps cereal

1 Tbsp lemon zest, grated

Cooking spray

Directions:

Use cooking spray to coat a loaf pan then heat 3 tbsps of unsalted butter on medium until melted. Add fine salt and 4 cups of mini marshmallows then stir until they melt. Add 3 cups of puffed rice then move the mixture to a pan. Use a spatula to press the mixture down.

Repeat the first step twice after rinsing the saucepan then add food coloring and orange zest before adding the cereal. Add yellow food color and lemon zest then press it down to the pan.

Let the mixture set for 2 hours or more then invert the loaf using a pan on a chopping board. Cut the loaf into 10 slices with the use of a serrated knife. Cut crosswise in half then mold into candy corn shaped pieces.

Enjoy!

Welcome to the Graveyard Pie (Martha Stewart .com)

Ingredients:

½ cup unsalted butter, melted then cooled

16 pieces Graham Crackers, broken into pieces

1 cup softened chocolate ice cream

1 cup fun-sized chocolates

1 cup softened vanilla ice cream

20 pieces chocolate wafers

6 oval chocolate sandwich cookies

2 Tbsp chocolate chips, melted then cooled

1 cup chocolate candy bars, chopped roughly

12 candy skulls

Directions:

First, pre-heat the oven to 325 F then process graham crackers in a food processor until finely ground. Add butter and pulse until combined then press the mixture into the bottom of a pie plate and bake until crust is set and dry.

Using a wooden spoon, stir vanilla ice cream in a bowl then add candy bars together with ice cream mixture. Freeze for 20 minutes to an hour, or until firm.

Add chocolate ice cream and coconut candy bars on top of the layer of vanilla ice cream then freeze for at least an hour.

Then, put a dot of melted chocolate onto each end of the cookie half and let the candy skulls set. Ground the wafers in the food processor and spread on top of the pie then make some slits and add cookie halves.

Serve immediately and enjoy!

You Gotta Have Slime

Slime can be a fun part of your decorations or as a means to poke dirty fun and will make the celebration so gooey good! Here's how to make it.

How to make Slime

You will need:

White glue

Water

Food coloring (preferably green, orange, black, or blue)

Borax

Directions:

Mix water with a teaspoon of borax. Make sure to stir until it is dissolved. Then, mix white glue with water in another container together with your choice of food coloring.

Combine the two solutions together and keep on mixing so that the slime won't harden thoroughly. You can now make shapes out of it, if you want, or you can just leave it be.

Voila! Your slime is now ready!

NOTE: Make sure not to eat the slime and not to add it to food. It would also be best to keep it in a sealed bottle or container if you're not going to use it yet. Good Luck!

Halloween Party Themes for Adults

Hey, Halloween is not just for the kids! You can make it fun and exciting for you, too, by creating a Halloween Party for adults. Here are some themes to consider.

Hollywood Nights

Ask everyone to dress up to the nines, just like they do at the Awards Shows. You don't have to buy extra expensive clothes; there are many classic evening gowns to be found at Goodwill.

Give out awards, such as "Best Dressed", "Scarediest Cat", "Creepy Stare". Serve wine, cheese, fruits, and classy finger foods and you're all set. Oh, and don't forget to order Pizza, too—If it's good enough for Ellen at the Oscars, its good enough for you, right?

Arabian Nights

Dress up like Princess Jasmine from Aladdin. Decorate the house with carpets and flowy curtains. Keep some lamps on the sides, and serve Moroccan or Arabian-inspired dishes. You could add some fake snakes and lions, too!

A Masquerade Ball

What is the best thing about masquerades? You can have this air of mystery around you—and you wouldn't have to let anyone else know who you are, at least, not until revelation time! Dress up in Renaissance inspired ball gowns and tuxes, make use of intricately designed masks. Serve macaroons, wine, and Roast Chicken with baked potatoes! It'll surely be a night your guests won't forget.

Go Gothic

Decorate the house in black, with just a little while thrown in. Put cauldrons and chalkboards all around. Make use of ornate candles, lamps, and pedestal bowls. Serve wine, and write menus on the chalkboards. Dress up in lacy, frilly costumes, and use dark make-up.

The Corpse Bride

Take a cue from this Tim Burton masterpiece. Dress up in wedding gowns or wedding attire but make sure to keep your make up dark. Make use of gauzy cheesecloth to mimic spider webs, or those mummy covers. And don't forget to serve wine and a tall, layered, cake! If you have one, put the piano at the center of the house, too, and decorate the walls with bats and butterflies.

Halloween Food and Drinks for Adults

 And of course, make sure that the party is complete with these spooky good dishes and drinks that you can make by yourself!

Webby Bat Pasta (Martha Stewart .com)

Ingredients:

2 chicken sausages, pre-cooked

½ lb bow-tie pasta

1/8 tsp sugar

1 tsp olive oil

1 garlic clove, minced

Coarse salt

¼ tsp dried oregano

8 oz mozzarella cheese, cut into cubes

1 can whole tomatoes, peeled and pureed

¼ cup Parmesan cheese, grated

Directions:

First, pre-heat the oven to 400F.

Cook pasta according to what's on the package then set aside after draining.

Heat oil in a large saucepan over medium heat then add garlic and cook for a minute or until fragrant. Add oregano, tomatoes, and sugar then boil for around 5 to 8 minutes or until thick.

Add sausage, pasta, and half of the mozzarella then toss until well-combined. Top the dish with Parmesan and the rest of the mozzarella then bake for around 10 to 15 minutes or until browned and bubbly.

Serve and enjoy!

Curry in a Cauldron (Martha Stewart .com)

Ingredients:

For the stew:

1 can light coconut milk, unsweetened

1 can regular coconut milk, unsweetened

1 cup spinach

¾ cup fresh basil

12 oz skinless and boneless chicken breasts

12 oz skinless and boneless chicken thighs

1 medium zucchini, cut into quarters

Serrano chilies, for garnish

Freshly ground pepper

Coarse salt

Lime wedges

Rice mixed with squash

For the curry:

1 Tbsp lime zest, grated finely

2 Tbsp fresh lime juice

2 Tbsp fresh ginger, peeled and chopped

2 scallions, chopped

8 garlic cloves, minced

2 stalks fresh lemongrass, trimmed then chopped

½ cup fresh cilantro

3 serrano chilies, sliced

1 tsp coarse salt

1 tsp toasted whole black peppercorns

2 tsp toasted whole cumin seeds

2 Tbsp toasted whole coriander seeds

Directions:

You have to make the curry paste first. Use mortar and pestle to grind cumin, salt, peppercorns and coriander together with the rest of the curry ingredients until pasty. What's good is that you can use this for at least 3 months!

Then, puree the spinach, 5 tablespoons of the curry paste and a cup of regular milk to create the stew. Just keep the rest of the curry paste for future use.

Mix light and regular coconut milk together in a stockpot over high heat then after 5 minutes, reduce heat to medium. Add zucchini and cook for around 5 minutes or until slightly tender.

Add chicken, pepper, and salt then cook chicken and zucchini for another 5 minutes. Add serrano chilies and basil and serve with lime wedges and the rice and squash mixture.

Creepy Fingers and Toes (Martha Stewart .com)

Ingredients:

24 blanched almonds, cut in halves

red food coloring

1 pack active dry yeast

1 Tbsp sugar

2 cups warm water

1 large egg

2 Tbsp baking soda

1 Tbsp coarse salt

5 to 6 cups all purpose flour

Vegetable oil

Fried rosemary

Sea salt

Directions:

Use food coloring for the rounded end of the almonds to resemble nail polishes then pour 2 cups of water to the electric mixer bowl. Add yeast and sugar and stir until sugar is dissolved. Beat flour together with the yeast then add coarse salt and beat some more. Then, move the dough to a floured surface and knead.

Place the dough in a bowl and coat it with oil. Set aside for around an hour, covered.

Then, pre-heat the oven to 400F and boil water over high heat. Cut the dough into quarters then cut the first quarter to 12 pieces. Roll each piece until you form finger-shaped pieces. Make toes, too, but make sure that they are smaller than the fingers to make them look realistic. Poach fingers and toes for at least a minute then brush them with egg wash. You can make egg wash by beating an egg with a tablespoon of water. Score the knuckles by using a sharp knife. Do this for around 3 times.

Sprinkle rosemary and sea salt then push almond nails into the dough. Bake for around 12 to 15 minutes or until golden brown then let them cool before serving.

Bloody Berry Float (Martha Stewart .com)

Ingredients:

750 ml Apple Cider

4 cups grape juice

1 cup raspberry sorbet

½ cup lime juice

Directions:

Combine wine, grape juice, and lime juice together in a large pitcher then spoon sorbet into glasses.

Top the sorbet with the grape, lime, and wine mixture that you have made.

Serve and enjoy!

Eye Can See You Martini (Martha Stewart .com)

Ingredients:

2 oz vodka

2 green olives, stuffed with pimento

2 whole black peppercorns

2 dashes Peychaud's bitters

½ oz vermouth, dry

Directions:

Make sure that you push peppercorns into the pimento filling in the center of each olive. Place the olives in the bottom of martini glasses.

Then, put some ice inside a cocktail shaker until you reach half of it. Add vermouth and vodka and shake until strained.

Before serving, add bitters to the sides of the glass.

Enjoy!

Welcome to the Black Lagoon (Martha Stewart .com)

Ingredients:

2 oz Lemon and Rosemary Syrup

4 oz vodka

licorice ice cubes

2 tsp fresh lemon juice

Directions:

In a cocktail shaker, combine syrup, vodka, and juice and stir until well-combined.

Fill cocktail glasses with licorice ice cubes.

Then, divide the cocktail between two glasses after adding the seltzer.

Serve and enjoy!

Cider full of Shrunken Heads (Martha Stewart .com)

Ingredients:

2 Tbsp coarse salt

2 cups lemon juice

2 cups spiced rum

32 whole cloves

2 cans frozen lemonade concentrate, thawed

8 large apples

2 gallons apple cider

Directions:

Pre-heat oven to 250 F then mix salt and lemon juice together in a bowl.

Next, peel the apples and cut them in half. Then, remove core and seeds then carve faces on them with the use of a paring knife. Soak the apples in lemon mixture for 1 minute then drain with paper towels.

On a baking sheet, place the apples face side up and bake them until they're dried or golden brown, or for at least 90 minutes. Make use of cloves to make eye sockets.

Then, in a large punchbowl, mix rum, lemonade, and cider together and let the makeshift shrunken heads swim on top.

Enjoy!

Note from Melinda

I hope this book was able to help you understand what Halloween is all about, and to create enticing dishes, wonderful costumes, and creepy but awesome decorations that you can use for your Halloween celebrations. If you have, please be kind and leave me a nice review at Amazon. This will help others find my book and I would really appreciate it.

And as a "Thank You" for downloading this book, I would like to give you a copy of one of my other books" The Raw Deal. The Real Benefits of Eating Raw for Health and Weight Loss"
To get your free copy, just visit my website: www.melindarolf.com

About the Author

Melinda is an Amazon best selling author and mom of three

She is an avid cook, soapmaker, crocheter, loomer, and has written several books on these subjects under the ...Home Life Series, all of which are available from Amazon and other fine stores in paperback and e-book format.

Melinda lives with her husband, 3 children 2 dogs, a cat, and a yellow bellied turtle in Swanville, Maine

Other Books by Melinda Rolf

Other Books in the "Home Life" Series by Melinda Rolf

101 DIY Household Hacks

The Wheat Belly Lifestyle

Mason Jar Recipes

Prep Freeze Serve

Prep Freeze Serve Chicken

African Black Soap & How to Make It

How to Make Natural Handmade Soap

Loom Jewelry for Beginners

The Superfood Power Smoothie Book

Crockpot Recipes

Meatless Eating

MELT Your Pain Away

The Raw Deal: Raw Food Lifestyle

Inside Crochet

Clean Eating

Mason Jar Holiday Gift Ideas

Planning the Perfect Christmas

Paleo Christmas

Paleo Thanksgiving

Available at Amazon and other fine stores in e-book and paperback format

www.ingramcontent.com/pod-product-compliance
Lightning Source LLC
Chambersburg PA
CBHW050800290526
45792CB00008B/2259